BELINDA

BELINDA
The Forest How
Red Squirrel

PETER G. TRIMMING

The Book Guild Ltd

First published in Great Britain in 2016 by
The Book Guild Ltd
9 Priory Business Park
Wistow Road, Kibworth
Leicestershire, LE8 0RX
Freephone: 0800 999 2982
www.bookguild.co.uk
Email: info@bookguild.co.uk
Twitter: @bookguild

Typeset in Gill Sans

ISBN 978 1 91087 855 2

British Library Cataloguing in Publication Data.
A catalogue record for this book is available from the British Library.

Dedicated to the memory of

John Harris

For his tireless work in supporting and protecting the
Forest How red squirrel colony.

Contents

Introduction by Helen Butler MBE

Our native red squirrels are magic! They are compulsive and charismatic to watch and often referred to as 'time-wasters'. Who can resist watching their antics and not admire their agility?

I have been captivated since starting work with them in 1991 and can fully understand why Peter visits Forest How, the Isle of Wight and other places where there are red squirrels. Peter is not only a keen observer but a very good photographer as well, as you will see in this book.

I've had the pleasure of visiting beautiful Forest How and meeting John and Deb and also some of the red squirrels there. Sadly at the time of my visit the squirrelpox was evident, which I hadn't seen first-hand before. It is a devastating disease and distressing to witness.

Red squirrels are up against a huge challenge in the UK as the American greys not only outcompete our native reds but also pass on squirrelpox. Grey squirrels carry, but rarely contract the disease but it can go through a red squirrel population very fast and virtually wipe it out.

If the UK lost red squirrels to the American greys, it would be very sad for future generations who will not have the pleasure of seeing this endearing woodland mammal. Please support red squirrel groups in the UK and become a volunteer if possible. You will find it very rewarding.

Helen Butler MBE
Wight Squirrel Project & The IOW Red Squirrel Trust

Chapter 1 – Setting the Scene

For thousands of years, the red squirrel (Sciurus vulgaris) has called the Eskdale Valley, in western Cumbria, its home. In more recent times, the valley still provides a suitable environment, with the River Esk and its tributaries providing water, and many woods and forests, both pine and deciduous, giving food and shelter; and providing connecting corridors, enabling movements within and between the red squirrel colonies.

The coming of the 21st century has brought new challenges for the Cumbrian red squirrel, which now finds itself in the front line as the introduced grey squirrel (Sciurus carolinensis) continues its march northwards.

Forest How, on the edge of Eskdale Green, is a house built in 1870; located on the eastern edge of Silver Knott, part of Muncaster Fell. Situated at the foot of the fells, it is protected from the westerly storms, and looks out upon Eskdale Green from a slightly elevated position. Immediately to the west, just beyond a public bridleway which runs through the garden, is a row of six assorted mature pine trees. 'Mature' is a loose description as, to be fair, they are past their best, but still hang on in this rugged terrain. Slightly higher up the fellside is a lone pine, because of its elevation appearing the largest of all. Garden walls and mature silver birch link these locations together. North-west of Forest How, the fellside is largely overgrown with a combination of silver birch, rhododendron, and a few slender pine trees. Slightly further north of this location, and linked by a few isolated trees and a stone wall, lies a rock outcrop, which is flanked by trees including mature oak and holly.

To the east of Forest How, lies an area described on some maps as 'Forest Moss', which gives a clue as to how wet it is under foot. However, Foresthow Wood now covers this area, consisting of some mature pine trees (perhaps planted soon after the house was built), and a vast amount of silver birch (which seems to have seeded naturally) and rhododendron, with oak and hazel dotted around the perimeter. The areas just described form what is loosely termed as 'home of the Forest How Red Squirrels'.

To the north of Forest How, just beyond Irton Road, is the Miterdale Forest, which is largely coniferous, and beyond which lies Wasdale. To the south, beyond the River Esk, lies Knott End, a large wood containing areas of both coniferous and deciduous trees; home to another colony of red squirrels, protected, to the south, by barren fells.

Forest How had been run as a guest house for a number of years, with John and Deb Harris taking over the running in March 2011.

Within a few weeks, a red squirrel had been spotted on a bird feeder, which resulted in John putting out food for the squirrel, and starting to take what became a keen interest. Photographs subsequently showed this to be a lactating female, who eventually went by the name of Celia Stripey-tail. Over the months, other red squirrels started to appear.

My involvement began in 2012. I had seen John's photographs early in the year, but circumstances dictated that I could not visit until later in the year, so had a visit booked for early September. The opportunity to study a small colony of wild red squirrels seemed just too good to miss.

Forest How Guest House. Nature Wood is to the right.

Northern entrance to Forest How. Silver Knott is to the right.
The walls are 'squirrel highways'.

Forest How from the south. Wounded Soldier's pine tree is on the extreme left.

Neighbour Celia's paddock. Squirrel dreys have been located in trees to the right.

A typical scene in Foresthow Wood.

View towards Miterdale Forest, from Nature Wood.

Chapter 2 – Meeting the Forest How Squirrels

Just prior to my September 2012 visit, I had asked John how many squirrels lived near the guest house, and visited the garden. "About six to eight," was his reply. I arrived in Eskdale, for the first time in nearly ten years, and for the first time as a 'wildlife' photographer, with high hopes. I had been there for less than an hour when I met Celia Stripey-tail on the terrace. She posed, briefly, before rushing off towards her drey. So, all was going well.

I was on a learning curve, trying to understand the habits of individual squirrels, work out where they lived, and where and when I might expect to see them, and my four day visit laid the foundations for subsequent visits. I could only confirm sightings of four individual squirrels, but was able to successfully identify Celia Stripey-tail, 'Wounded Soldier' and 'Lady From the Wood'.

Colour, size, thickness of ear-tufts at the appropriate time of the year, and behaviour, all contributed towards identification of the individual squirrels. Also, having them sit up whilst eating, enabled identification as male or female. On my first visit, Celia

Stripey-tail had bands of dark brown and slightly lighter brown on her tail, but these had moulted out by the next year, and did not return.

Celia Stripey-tail had two tricks when it came to carrying food. Her head was slightly longer than those of the other squirrels, which enabled her to carry two hazelnuts if she carefully selected the sizes. Also, if she took a hazelnut in her mouth, and a peanut at the side of the mouth, this was a clue that she was about to return to her drey.

Subsequent visits in October 2012, and January/February 2013 saw me making further progress, and building trust with the squirrels. The January/February visits saw me photographing squirrels in the snow; fun, and a rare occurrence in Eskdale because of the low altitude and proximity to the sea. A mid-June visit, in a heatwave, saw Wounded Soldier still in his winter coat, and Lady From the Wood lactating. It had been a long, cold, winter, and everything seemed to be happening late. My mid-August visit saw cooler (normal) temperatures, and Wounded Soldier in his summer coat. The colour change, from blonde to almost black tail was stunning, however his torn left ear confirmed that it was the same squirrel. This visit also saw Nutkin, a young male squirrel, make his first appearance.

John and I attended a Conservation Day meeting at Dalegarth Station, in October 2013. We were asked to estimate the number of squirrels at Forest How. I pitched the number at a slightly conservative twelve, taking into account all of the 'named' squirrels, plus others which we had seen on an occasional basis. People might think it madness to name wild animals; however, it certainly aids identification when coupled with photographic evidence.

Celia Stripey-tail, 17th August 2013, showing her head profile.

Mr. Tail to the Right, a resident in 2013; 22nd January.

Tracks by Celia Stripey-tail, 22nd January 2013.
Note rear paws landing outside front paws.

Wounded Soldier, 18th June 2013.

Wounded Soldier, 19th August 2013.

Lady From the Wood, 18th May 2014.

Nutkin, 31st October 2013.

Chapter 3 – Disaster Strikes

Looking at maps and an aerial view of the area around Forest How, all logic suggested that the red squirrel density was higher than might have been expected. It was almost an 'accident waiting to happen', John and I agreed when we looked back on what had happened. Young squirrels generally disperse in the autumn, to find their own territories. Their needs are simple; food, water and shelter. They are generally solitary animals, and only tolerate other related squirrels. There was a bumper nut crop in 2014, excellent news for squirrels. However, the previous autumns were not so plentiful, and I concluded (rightly or wrongly) that more squirrels chose to live near the guest house to benefit from the supplementary food put out on a daily basis.

In May 2014, I arrived at Forest How in a heatwave which lasted for a couple of months, during which time there was virtually no rain. The squirrels were happy, despite the weather, coming regularly for food, and posing nicely for visiting photographers. The squirrels were living in the following locations:

North-west of the guest house: Celia Stripey-tail (the dominant female, aged at least four but probably five years), plus her daughter born in March 2014.

West of the guest house, in the row of six pine trees: Nutkin in the first tree; Nigel, Tumbler (plus her kittens) in the second tree.

West of the guest house, in the lone pine: Wounded Soldier (now the dominant male).

East of the guest house, in Foresthow Wood: Lady From the Wood (plus her kittens), Nick, plus several un-named squirrels.

On my arrival, I was concerned to hear that the red squirrel colony, less than a mile south of Forest How, at Linbeck at the foot of Knott End, had seen the arrival of the squirrelpox virus. From what I had read, when this strikes a red squirrel colony, fatality rates can be as high as 97%. I kept my fingers crossed, but feared the worst.

Back home, in early June, I had a worried telephone call from John, who was watching a poorly Nigel trying to climb up to his drey, and had taken some photographs of Wounded Soldier, who did not look good. I feared squirrelpox, but the pictures did not show the terrible scabs around the eyes and other areas which I had seen on squirrel websites. The next day, John found Nigel dead under his drey, and later in the day saw a very poorly Wounded Soldier, who he managed to trap and took the sad decision to put him out of his misery. John sprayed disinfectant everywhere but, as he said, "You can't spray the branches of the trees."

Two trips over the mountains, that day, saw John deliver each of the bodies to a vet, who was to urgently arrange a post-mortem. Within days, the results confirmed that both squirrels had the squirrelpox virus. Subsequent days brought worse news; Nutkin had the virus, as had Celia Stripey-tail. John managed to trap Celia Stripey-tail, and nursed her to the end in a large cage which he had constructed. Experts normally expect an infected squirrel to die within 10-14 days. From the first indication that Celia had a problem (slightly inflamed teat), she lasted 27 or 28 days. We concluded that she had some resistance to the virus, but not enough to see her through. Maybe age was against her. During the squirrelpox outbreak, John spoke to dozens of experts; in the hope that he might be able to prevent the complete loss of the colony.

My planned June visit was delayed until July, as I did not really want to see sick and dying squirrels. However, my mid-July visit was not a happy one. I saw Lady From the Wood at a distance, running well along a wall. However, a poor quality photograph showed scabs around her eye. We never did see her again, nor find her body. Sick, un-named, squirrels were coming out of the wood; squirrels which we had never seen before. Still the heatwave continued, and the virus can remain viable, in these conditions, for 30 days. I saw Celia's Daughter, during the squirrelpox outbreak, but feared the worst. I had seen her with

Mum, during my May visit, when she was aged only eight weeks; large for her age, and probably the only surviving kitten from her 2014 litter.

I left for home, feeling depressed, and wondering how John must have been feeling. The final list of casualties was 12 adults and 1 juvenile; 8 males, 4 females, and 1 not checked. That was the known casualties.

Fellside trees. Nutkin's drey was in the tree to the right.
Squirrels move between trees, high above the ground.

Arriving in the summer of 2013, the hollow logs were an instant hit with the squirrels.

Squirrel suffering with squirrelpox, 13th July 2014.

Chapter 4 – Lone Squirrel

The squirrelpox outbreak, at Forest How, had lasted for all of June and July 2014. In the latter part of August, I telephoned John Harris. "Well, I've got one squirrel ... and he seems healthy!" was his response to my question. I sensed a combination of relief, and sadness in his voice. One squirrel was obviously better than none, but not much use on its own.

I was due to visit in early September, a trip which had been booked more than a year previously. My plans, with a probable lack of squirrels, had been to carry out woodland maintenance, in the hope that some squirrels had survived. Back in July, John had shown two of us (Helen Butler was visiting on her way back to the Isle of Wight) what was to become known as 'Nature Wood'; part of the land owned by Forest How. We had found an old squirrel drey in a holly tree, proving that squirrels had, at some stage, been present in this small wood.

Immediately prior to my visit, John advised that there must be more than one squirrel, due to the amount of nuts vanishing (mostly un-seen). So, my first task would be to establish the facts. Soon after arriving, my first evening saw me staking out two locations; with a video camera running at one. Before long, I had the proof; a wood mouse at each location. I had a nice video clip of one mouse running off with a hazelnut, and managed a photograph of a second at the other location. So, that left us still with just one known squirrel.

Bill, as he became known, showed up on the next morning. We quickly established that he did not really like humans. We subsequently found that he was not overly fond of other squirrels either.

A couple of days later, I had completed my first phase of clearance in Nature Wood, opening up paths which had not been used in some 30 years. Limbs of gorse, up to four inches in diameter, and ten feet long, were removed and piled up.

Beside the guest house, I was regularly checking a large beech tree, in the hope of seeing one specific squirrel. Celia Stripey-tail had died during the squirrelpox outbreak, but her elusive offspring, named Celia's Daughter had been seen in this tree, with mother, in mid-May. Aged only eight weeks at the time, and a large squirrel for her age, she had been mapping the tree whilst Mum looked on. Celia's Daughter had been active during my July visit, but all we had was brief sightings, followed by the sound of hazelnuts being opened and eaten in the hedgerow, so we had not been able to check on her health. Finally, early on 6th September, I spotted her high up in the beech tree. So, there were definitely two squirrels.

Two squirrels quickly became three. I returned to Nature Wood, where a rock outcrop, known as 'Peter's Viewpoint', gave good views down into the wood. A mature oak tree covered the location, but the rock outcrop put the observer up in the tree canopy. I knew that roe deer used this wood (in fact, two had run out when I entered a couple of days previously), and thought that the viewpoint would also be ideal for bird observation, and squirrels, should they re-populate the wood. I had literally just completed this thought, when I saw movement in a tree. It was a still day, and the movement seemed excessive for a bird. As I watched, I could see that it was, indeed, a squirrel; some 50 yards away. As we subsequently discovered, there were two hazel trees on the edge of the wood. The squirrel was harvesting the nuts and burying them in the adjacent field. After a while, it moved from the small hazel tree into a larger one. I took a chance, and worked my way down to a stone wall, at the edge of the wood, and close to the second hazel tree. I was finally seen, and off went the squirrel, back into the nearby Foresthow Wood.

The next morning saw me back in Nature Wood, only this time with a camera. The pattern of the previous day was repeated, only this time I hid behind the wall and waited. Eventually, the squirrel came along the wall, hazelnuts in mouth, saw me, let out a cry, climbed up the nearest tree, swished its tail, and looked down at me. Amazingly, one picture out of three was sharp, and I had a good enough view to establish that Lucky was female, before I departed. A very positive 60th Birthday!

A subsequent exploration of Foresthow Wood revealed a line of nut trees bordering the railway line. So, we concluded that Lucky's range was long and narrow, and she had probably survived by avoiding contact with the squirrelpox virus.

Bill, in Foresthow Wood, 15th June 2015.

Lucky, in Nature Wood, 7th September 2014.

Beech tree near the guest house. A squirrel 'magnet' in early autumn 2014.

'Peter's Viewpoint', Nature Wood.

View from 'Peter's Viewpoint'. Note the nest box. An old drey was found nearby.

Chapter 5 – Homes for Squirrels

During the 'dark' days of August 2014, John had started building a batch of squirrel nest boxes, based on a design which he had obtained from a friend. Whether they would be successful was open to debate, but the theory was sound. The entry point was to be a diameter of 2 inches, reinforced by a metal collar; too small for an adult grey squirrel to enter, and impossible for a grey squirrel to chew around the hole to enlarge it. So, a safe haven for red squirrels; with no twigs to cause cuts around the eyes, a possible entry point for the squirrelpox virus (one of several ways in which the red squirrel is thought to contract the virus).

John had shown me the almost completed first batch of boxes at the start of September. With news that the squirrel count had reached three, John finished the first batch of boxes with renewed enthusiasm, and we were soon attaching the first three to trees in Nature Wood. I say 'we', but John did virtually all of the work; I just helped to carry a very heavy ladder, and stood by to record the events for posterity.

Each squirrel box had a 'starter kit' of dried moss and sheep's fleece, with choice of décor left to each individual squirrel. We were confident that, eventually, squirrels would use some of the boxes, if they were in the right place at the right time of the year. Examination of bird nest boxes, at the end of the summer, had shown that a squirrel had previously nested in an owl nest box, and two smaller bird boxes sported enlarged entrances. We had previously photographed a squirrel sitting in an open-fronted bird box, lower down on a tree than we would have anticipated.

Visitors to Forest How Guest House were happy to sponsor a 'box for life' and, as the months progressed, squirrel nest boxes were starting to appear in all of the woods surrounding Forest How. Squirrels were seen checking them out, and we know, for certain, that great tits occupied two of the boxes.

First batch of squirrel nest boxes, 4th September 2014.

Off to Nature Wood, with the first squirrel nest boxes.

John with squirrel nest box. Fellside, overlooking Forest How.

Squirrel's view towards Forest How.

Squirrel investigating a nest box, 27th October 2014.

Fellside squirrel nest box. Each box was placed as high as was practical.

Chapter 6 – A New Star Appears

Late summer and early autumn 2014 produced a bumper nut crop. As a result, there was no need for squirrels to regularly visit Forest How for a top-up of hazelnuts, peanuts and seeds.

My early September visit was closely followed by another, at the end of the month, to take in the annual Eskdale Show. Between these two visits, I checked with John Harris for an update on the squirrel situation. John had set up a feeder, on the edge of Nature Wood, at the location where I had seen Lucky, and hazelnuts were going at a steady rate.

John reported seeing two squirrels having a chase around the nearest large pine tree in the garden. He initially thought that both were male, but photographs only proved conclusive on the darker squirrel which we had seen from August onwards. I named them Bill and Ben. However, when I arrived in late September, it soon became obvious that I needed a female name, so it became Bill and Belinda. As luck would have it, within a couple of days, a Ben had also turned up!

Mark, another photographer, who was staying at the guest

house on a long-term business trip, had spent the previous day, when John and I were away, hiding in the bracken in full camouflage. His success rate with the squirrels was virtually nil. Mark and I watched Bill aggressively chase Belinda up, down, and around the nearby large pine tree. Once, they briefly stopped; one on either side of the tree, listening for sounds of movement from the other squirrel. I took the opportunity to talk to the squirrels. As Belinda looked towards me, I asked her whether she wanted a hazelnut, and held an arm out wide to show her the nut. Her gaze went from me, towards the nut. "She will be the one to pose," I confidently predicted. The chase then recommenced. Up and down the tree, again, noisily, then through the next four conifer trees, at full speed, then along a section of stone wall heading up the fellside. They continued up into Wounded Soldier's old pine tree; up, down, and around. We could hear shouts and squeals as they continued the chase, still in the pine tree, then through a line of mature silver birch. Finally, it went quiet.

After quite a few minutes, Belinda was the one to return. She was soon hoovering up the nuts and seeds on offer at a couple of feeding locations.

The next day, I set up another feeding position, and positioned the video camera accordingly. Down came Belinda, happy to take nuts only about four feet from me. Mark was there with his camera, and the loud sequence of shutter clicks suggested that he was doing much better than previously. I was happy to 'invest in the future' by supplying nuts and giving Belinda suitable encouragement.

A day later, Bill was again chasing Belinda, but not with the same measure of success. Ben then arrived, and Belinda chased him out of the large pine tree. I concluded that Belinda had decided to stake her claim for this part of the fellside, and was prepared to defend it.

My visit ended on the 2nd of October, and photographs taken towards the end of the visit show Belinda giving the nicest poses of the three visible squirrels. The elusive Celia's Daughter and Lucky may have been seen, fleetingly, but were certainly not photographed.

So, Belinda, the new star, had arrived and was making quite an impression. I managed to track her on her foraging circuit. She was living deep in Foresthow Wood, working her way through the garden and into the line of pine trees on the lower fellside. Next stop was to check the feeding locations; any food there was either eaten, or removed and cached. When the food ran out, she would move along to the large beech tree; very much a squirrel magnet, often with two squirrels in it. She would then continue along the tree line, cross the track behind the horse box, climb up the nearest oak tree in the paddock, and make her way back into Foresthow Wood via the garden. One morning, I watched her complete this circuit three times; each time, we delayed her at the feeding locations.

We will never know for certain whether Belinda was born in Foresthow Wood, but it seems likely that she was deep in the wood whilst the squirrelpox was raging. In appearance and colour, she reminded me of Lady From the Wood who had successfully bred for at least three years. Sometimes, she reminded me of Wounded Soldier, who was the dominant male. So, I have speculated that she might well have been the offspring of this pair.

Just before my May 2014 visit, John had seen a female bring out several juveniles from the direction of Foresthow Wood, to show them where to find food. We know that two other females which bred in the spring were not based in the wood, so it is a reasonable assumption that Lady From the Wood was the mother seen. We never did find her body, but a slightly out of focus picture, taken in July 2014, showed a very active squirrel, but with signs of squirrelpox around her right eye.

A hyperactive Belinda was now around to continue the Forest How legacy.

Belinda. First picture, 29ᵗʰ September 2014.

Belinda, 1ˢᵗ October 2014.

Belinda, getting more relaxed; 1st October 2014.

Belinda, checking a new feeding location; 2nd October 2014.

Chapter 7 – Squirrel Training

My late October visit saw squirrel foraging continue, but the large beech tree, now devoid of nuts, was no longer a squirrel magnet. Celia's Daughter and Bill made fleeting visits to the garden most days, but only stayed for a few minutes, indicating that food in the wood was still plentiful.

For the same reason, I did not see Lucky, and cannot say for certain whether Ben visited. On two days, I saw a uniform dark brown squirrel which I could not identify, so this was probably a 'new' squirrel.

Belinda, however, was an absolute star. Visiting every day as part of her foraging routine, if food was available, she would hide it as soon as possible, returning for more when John or myself were visible. She was manic, and I have never seen a squirrel work so hard, hiding food in a wide range of locations. Her tail, which had been quite a light colour, was turning darker, apart from a blonde tip. This was very useful, when trying to track her progress on the fellside.

I had wondered whether it might be possible for Belinda to take nuts from the hand, as she was by far the most friendly and confident squirrel. One morning, when I made Belinda aware that I had hazelnut kernels in my hand, I crouched low on the damp grass. Belinda came close, and started circling around me; much to the amusement of John, who was standing at a safe distance. Round and round she went, looking at the nuts, wanting them, and working out how to get them. Finally, she started creeping towards my outstretched hand. When she got there, she started nibbling the end of my finger. "That's my finger!" I said, and the nibbling stopped. Obviously, with the eyes of a squirrel set at the side of the head, close work is done by smell. A puzzled Belinda was probably thinking "If it smells like a hazelnut, it probably is a hazelnut." She tried again, with the same result. On the third try, she put her paws on my hand, and found the hazelnut kernels. She took the nuts, and ran off with her prize, before returning for more.

We never did work out whether the 'squirrel training' was me training Belinda, or her training me. Either way, both parties seemed happy with the outcome.

Belinda can obviously recognise different humans as, one morning, she came up to the conservatory window, and peered in at me whilst I was having my breakfast. The squirrels normally just grab a nut and run off.

Outside, Belinda would come for food wherever I would sit or stand. Mostly, she would run off and bury the nuts, but a couple of times sat just six inches away to eat. When strange sounds, or other people approaching, brought out her natural caution, she climbed up a nearby tree, but soon returned when it was quiet. Whilst I did not get her to pose on my leg, as I sat on the log, she twice came up from behind and put a paw on me (the second time, John photographed this).

Between bouts of entertaining the photographers at the feeding locations, Belinda found time to pose in the trees on the fellside as a 'normal' squirrel. I also found her working on a nest during one wet day; fit for purpose, as it was in the decayed wood of one of the large pine trees, close to the feeding locations, and kept the worst of the weather away from her, but little more than two feet above ground level.

Belinda nibbling Peter's fingers, 26th October 2014.

Belinda asking her friend for more nuts, 26th October 2014.

Belinda's nest, lower fellside. I filmed her working on this, on 28th October 2014.

Belinda's nest location. Close to the ground, but also close to the food.

Belinda and John, 28th October 2014. Belinda willing the hazelnut to move closer.

Chapter 8 – Flying Squirrel

John and I had discussed the possibility of 'flying squirrel' pictures, however we had not really come up with a suitable location and, of course, we needed the all-important squirrel. When I arrived at the end of November, for my last visit of the year, I boldly announced to John how we would get the pictures. In Belinda, we had the squirrel which seemed happy to rise to all of our challenges, and I had worked out the take-off point. All we needed was a suitable landing position.

Deep in his workshop, John found the ideal item; an old tripod which soon had a wooden landing platform attached. The next morning saw the tripod placed about four feet from one of the feeding positions, and a little further down the slope. Nuts were placed on the landing platform, and a small branch used to link the take-off and landing positions. We then awaited the return of Belinda.

It worked exactly as planned, with Belinda running along the branch to gather the hazelnuts. After a couple of visits, I removed the branch and Belinda, with no hesitation, jumped across the gap to reach the nuts, returning to her take-off point just a few seconds later. That was the easy part; getting pictures which were sharp, and included the whole squirrel, proved more of a challenge, especially as her take-off point varied by a critical few inches. John and I worked as a team, one as the 'spotter' with a telephoto lens and camera on a tripod, the other lying on the ground, with a pre-focussed 50mm lens on the camera, waiting for the call of "Here she comes!"

On and off, Belinda kept us entertained for over two and a half hours, interrupted occasionally by a chase involving one of the male squirrels. Due to the time of year, and available daylight, our pictures were not perfect; however, we had proved that the process would work for us.

My visit saw the squirrel, seen fleetingly during the previous month, formally introduced as Belle. Also Lucky was finally seen, leaving Nature Wood, after a couple of near misses on previous days. Like Belinda, she had also developed a blonde tip to her tail, but her body fur had become darker.

On my final morning, I was relaxing in the garden, just prior to leaving. Belinda spotted me, climbed up onto the table where I had my coffee, and relieved me of my last few hazelnuts, before we went our separate ways.

'Flying' squirrel set-up, 30ᵗʰ November, 2014.

Airborne Belinda, 30ᵗʰ November, 2014.

In-coming Belinda, 30th November 2014.

Belinda returning with hazelnut, 30th November 2014.

Chapter 9 – Moving Home

With my next visit being in late January 2015, I wondered what changes had occurred within the red squirrel colony. Belle was seen on a daily basis, and a new squirrel called Beatrix, who had a recent scar to the right side of her nose, but otherwise looked very similar to Belle, was also in evidence. Lucky was not seen, but nuts were still leaving her feeder on an occasional basis. Bill and Ben were about, but where was Belinda?

John had seen Belinda on the day of my arrival, but it was almost three days before I finally saw her. It was then 'back to normal', although Belinda now always seemed to appear from the fellside, rather than from Foresthow Wood, leading me to speculate that she had moved her main drey. As it would be approaching the breeding season, and squirrels can breed from the age of eleven months, I speculated that Belinda was changing her thoughts towards family matters. One day I saw her heading south of the guest house gardens, onto the fellside, no doubt looking for suitable trees.

Belinda proved both the most industrious of the squirrels, plus the quickest to learn. John and I used a variety of feeding locations; in the garden, orchard, Foresthow Wood, on the fellside etc. Every time that Belinda found food in a new location, she included that location within her foraging route, just in case more food had been left. She cached her food everywhere and, with much more blonde visible in her tail, was easy to track.

Squirrel dynamics were becoming clear. When Celia's Daughter was visiting, Belinda kept out of her way. Belinda seemed to hold her own with the male squirrels, but chased Belle when she appeared. Interestingly, Belle seemed to be favouring a large oak tree, where the owl nest box was located. I set up a camera trained on the nest box to see whether Belle went inside. John was aware of the setup, and ready to start filming if I was not around. As a result, John filmed Belle and Belinda in an aggressive chase up, down and around this tree. However; it was Belle doing all the chasing, so we concluded that she had staked her claim to this tree.

Beatrix, 20th January 2015.

Belle, 20th January 2015.

Belinda in the orchard, 20th January 2015.
The right branch was lost in a winter gale.

Belinda, 22nd January 2015.

Chapter 10 – Family Planning

Before I arrived in mid-February, John had advised that it might be hard work, as his sightings had been well down in previous weeks. However; the advantage of having unlimited time, ensured that almost all possible sightings were recorded.

John had been seeing an unfamiliar, shy, squirrel in days prior to my arrival. He turned out to be a male squirrel, named Bertie, who must have moved into the area. An early arrival, most mornings, and very hungry, we deduced that he did not have a food cache from the autumn.

The sightings summary for the visit was as follows:

Bill – Fri/Sun – total 2.
Ben – Sat/Sun/Tue – total 3.
Bertie – Fri/Sun/Mon/Tue/Wed/Thu – total 6.
Belle – Fri/Sat/Sun/Mon/Tue/Wed/Thu – total 7.
Beatrix – Fri – total 1.
Belinda – Fri/Sun/Mon/Tue/Thu – total 5.
Celia's Daughter – Sun/Tue – total 2.
Lucky – not seen.

In terms of squirrel locations (home drey), these appeared to be as follows:

In Foresthow Wood (east/south-east of the guest house):
Bertie, Belle, Beatrix.

On the fellside (west/north-west of the guest house):
Bill, Ben, Belinda, Celia's Daughter.

Their ranges overlapped in the Forest How Guest House gardens, and the nearby lower fellside.

The 'odd one out' was Lucky. Initially she was seen on the boundary of Nature Wood and Foresthow Wood, to the north-east of the guest house. We speculated that this was the northern limit of her range. There are many nut trees on the edge of Foresthow Wood, beside the railway line. Therefore, her range was very narrow, and probably long, running along a north-west to south-east axis.

A red squirrel, possibly Lucky, was seen at the south-eastern corner of Foresthow Wood in late January/early February. Soon afterwards, there was another sighting at the south-eastern edge of Bankend Wood. This is a mainly coniferous wood, linked to Foresthow Wood by a ribbon of silver birch and nut trees. I was not aware of other red squirrels in this wood, so this could have been the southern limit of her range, or she may have moved into Bankend Wood.

Bearing in mind that it was the time of year when the squirrels could be involved in mating chases, I saw very little activity. My notes indicated Ben chasing Belle on 17th February, but I saw no activity involving Belinda. However, Belinda was not seen on two days, which was unusual, so I speculated that any chasing may have occurred further along the fellside. I had seen the red squirrel pregnancy period being variously quoted as between 35 and 38 days, so these figures are probably a good guide.

Belinda on a fellside tree, 13th February 2015. A location popular with the squirrels.

Belinda on the fellside log, 13th February 2015.

Belinda in the garden, 17th February 2015, just outside the kitchen.

Chapter 11– Surprise News

Early March brought some unwelcome news; a squirrel turned up, showing the signs of squirrelpox. John took some photographs which sadly confirmed the situation, and had the task of catching the squirrel and putting him out of his misery. This turns out to have been Bertie, but we had no idea how or where he had picked up the virus.

I arrived at Forest How in mid-March, fearing the worst after the horrors of 2014. However, there was surprise news in that both Belinda and Belle were lactating. They were showing no signs of pregnancy in mid-February, so I put the birth dates as very early March. This explained the lack of mating chases during my February visit, since they would have occurred towards the end of January!

I did manage to both see, and follow, Celia's Daughter as she left the gardens to return to her drey via two stone walls. I concluded that she was either staying in, or very near to, her mother's old drey which we had discovered in a holly tree, north-west of the guest house, during our extensive searches of early September 2014.

Ben was seen, briefly, on two days of the visit. Luckily, I caught him on video, facing the camera. Frame by frame analysis gave just two or three frames proving that he was a male, and then I noticed some patchy fur on his face, which nicely corresponded with some photographs taken on the previous visit. Early one morning, I spotted a squirrel coming out of Foresthow Wood, using the gate and wall to access the fellside. It was not one of the females so was either Bill or Ben, suggesting a larger home range than I had previously recorded.

Squirrel activity was down on previous months, but with young kittens to feed, the two mothers were spending more time back at their dreys.

Another surprise was Belinda, departing one day and taking exactly the same route as Celia's Daughter had done a couple of days previously. So, the two squirrels were near neighbours.

Thinking ahead, and realising that my April visit would see spring flowers limiting my photographic opportunities in the garden, I set up a new feeding position on the lower fellside. I left a hazelnut on top, and checked back on a daily basis. Even the smart Belinda took three days to find it, but that was another location added to her foraging route.

Belinda, 16th March 2015.

Belinda, 16th March 2015.

Belinda at the new fellside feeding location, 17ᵗʰ March 2015.

Belinda on the fellside, 20ᵗʰ March 2015.

The new fellside feeding location.

Route back to the dreys. Celia's Daughter and Belinda were seen running along the walls.

The blown-down tree in Foresthow Wood. Regularly used by Belle and Belinda.

Ben, on the garden wall; 29th August 2015. Belinda seemed happy for him to be around.

Chapter 12 – Spring Days

My visit, towards the end of April, brought temperatures lower than those of March. Squirrel sightings were down but, interestingly, Belinda seemed to be spending more time back in Foresthow Wood. This led me to speculate that she might move back into this wood when her kittens became independent.

Both Belinda and Belle were using a very natural feeding location in Foresthow Wood. This was a tree; blown down by a winter gale, and leaning against a huge pine tree, but still alive. Both squirrels were part way through the moult into their summer coat, so were looking a bit scruffy.

One magical moment involved Belinda on a log in the garden. I had scattered a few pieces of hazelnut in the usual position. Belinda arrived, hazelnut in mouth, to check out the location. In one photograph, it is possible to see her looking at the pieces of nut. She then took the hazelnut out of her mouth, set it down, ate the hazelnut pieces, picked up the nut again, and ran off.

One afternoon, I filmed both Belinda and Belle, in rotation, on the feeding position in Foresthow Wood, ending with Belinda doing some chasing before both rested up in different trees. Early the next morning saw me back at the same location, this time to take photographs. I was photographing Belle from 06:30 for some ten minutes, before she departed and Belinda arrived from the depths of Foresthow Wood.

06:45 saw Belinda in place, happily eating the hazelnut pieces as I crouched low for a better angle. A minute later, I was distracted by the sound of irate blackbirds. Looking up, I saw two male blackbirds chasing a tawny owl straight towards me! The owl passed so close that, had I raised my hand, I would have touched its wing. I looked back, and Belinda was nowhere to be seen. The owl had landed in a nearby tree, but when I looked again, it was gone; no doubt chased off by the blackbirds. I turned back to the feeding location to see Belinda emerging, nut in mouth, to check that the coast was clear. This proved the value of having feeding locations where there is either cover for the squirrels, or an easy escape route.

John had seen a squirrel whilst I had both Belle and Belinda with me in Foresthow Wood, so we concluded that this was the elusive Celia's Daughter, and who was also seen by Rob, another visiting photographer, on a previous day.

Belinda on the fellside, 27th April, 2015.
Her teats show that she was probably still lactating.

Belinda spotting hazelnut pieces, 25th April 2015.

Belinda in Foresthow Wood, 27th April 2015. Mid moult, the lighter fur was her winter coat.

Belinda resting, post-hazelnuts, 27th April 2015.

Belinda at 06:45, 30th April 2015. Prior to the arrival of a tawny owl.

Belinda at 06:46, 30th April 2015. After the owl had passed.

Chapter 13 – Where are the Squirrels?

My late May visit had been booked in the hope of seeing the first sightings of juvenile squirrels. When I arrived, my first sighting was a shock. Belle was still mid moult, looking scruffy and a bit poorly. She also had a cough. "She's been like that for about two weeks," said John. Concerned that she may have contracted squirrelpox, I kept a close watch whenever she appeared. Her eyes looked fine, with absolutely no trace of a problem. There was, however, a mark on her lower mouth in exactly the same place as we had seen on Wounded Soldier the previous year. There was also a bare patch on her right flank, where an old tick bite was visible.

Belle did not appear every day, but food continued to vanish, and she seemed to improve during the week. The dilemma before us was discussed. If Belle had squirrelpox, it was probable that she had passed it on to her kittens. She was in regular contact with Belinda, who probably already had the virus if she was going to catch it. All the other squirrels had seemed to have vanished. Had they died, moved out of the location, or were they finding sufficient food in the woods not to require a visit? Rightly or wrongly, we decided to let nature take its course. Towards the end of my visit, Belle was well enough to be chased by Belinda, up and down a tree, and deep into Foresthow Wood.

Belinda seemed in the best of health, and was bounding around like a youngster. Up early for foraging, and staying out later, she was spending much time in Foresthow Wood. One evening, I was still photographing her at 20:00, as lovely warm sunshine flooded through the wood.

One day I saw Belinda taking a bundle of moss up into one of the pine trees overlooking the guest house. I checked the tree as best I could, but no drey was visible. I concluded, therefore, that there was a nest high up, in a hollow part of the tree, and that a refurbishment was under way.

On another day, I saw Belinda on the largest pine tree in Foresthow Wood, in which Lady From the Wood had a drey in early 2013. She was clearly thinking of moving in, checking out her squirrel chase moves on the three huge, vertical, branches. Round and round the left branch she danced, playing chase with an imaginary squirrel. She then turned to face down, and again danced around. Turning around, again, she then jumped from the left branch to the right branch, a distance of at least six feet, and carried on her dance. After a while, she sat on a horizontal branch and groomed herself, as she was suffering badly with fleas and ticks.

Belinda was being very industrious, again, carrying hazelnuts to all corners of the garden, the wood, and the fellside. One morning, I estimated that she cleared in excess of forty hazelnuts. She posed nicely, a few times, and took nuts from my hand on most days. Being a very smart squirrel, she had also found out where the hazelnuts were stored. When they were lacking in all the normal feeding locations, she could be seen emerging from the back yard with a nut in her mouth.

In between times, I planted a small rowan (which had come from Nature Wood in September 2014), and three hazel saplings which had been donated to John. Their new location being at the edge of the garden, on the boundary with the fellside. Whilst Belinda might not see the benefit, it is to be hoped that her offspring will still be in the area when the first nuts ripen.

I had been checking two other nearby locations, where red squirrel sightings had been reported. On the edge of Bankend Wood, nuts were disappearing daily between late evening and mid-morning. The second location was beside Thwaite Wood, where a bridge crossed the River Esk. As I approached, one morning, I saw a red squirrel breaking cover, leaving the edge of Thwaite Wood for some gorse bushes which gave cover all the way up to Bankend Wood. It was not the squirrel which I was hoping to see, as the orange/red colour was brighter than any recently seen at Forest How. It was, however, a red squirrel.

Belinda in Foresthow Wood, 23rd May 2015.

Belinda on the 'squirrel highway', 25th May 2015. First picture at this location.

Belinda on the fellside log, 25th May 2015. Black colour forming in her tail fur.

Belinda in Foresthow Wood, 27th May 2015.
Feeding happily on my observation seat.

Looking across Foresthow Wood. The tallest pine tree has been favoured by the squirrels. In January 2013, Lady From the Wood had a drey at the top.

Chapter 14 – Class of 2015 Arrives

John rang me at the start of June, excited that he had seen Belinda with her two youngsters that afternoon. So, the timing of my previous visit was out by about four days. Another visit was booked and, the day before I was due to arrive, John rang again to say that he had seen six juvenile squirrels that day. This was a puzzle, since we knew that Belinda had two, and presumed that Belle had two. Whilst it is possible for larger litters, two or three kittens seem to be the norm. Could Celia's Daughter also have two? A quick calculation proved that this was just possible.

My visit brought several surprises. The bad news was no sightings of Belle since five days after my May visit, when John caught her on camera. So, if it was squirrelpox, she had survived for more than three weeks. Several juvenile squirrels were seen during my visit, possibly as many as six. Bill and Ben were back, and a lactating Beatrix was seen, although she had a bit of a cough.

Belinda's youngsters were fairly easy to identify, as they were similar in colour to her. She had a very bold male, and a rather cute female who posed really nicely.

Celia's Daughter did, indeed, have two kittens. A male was identified and named as Celia's Grandson, and possibly a female. The male had slightly darker fur on his head and back, making him easy to identify when playing with Belinda's youngsters. One day, as John and I watched, one of Celia's Daughter's youngsters climbed into a large pine tree, and sat close behind her on the same branch.

Belle's youngsters, and I think I saw both, were a darker brown; just like Mum, in the autumn of 2014. I was on the lookout for squirrelpox, and sadly found it in the right eye of the male. The decision was taken that if he became more lethargic, he would sadly have to be removed from the colony, which happened only two days after I first saw him.

I had concluded that Belinda and Celia's Daughter had been near neighbours to the north-west of the guest house, so it is just possible that, as kittens, the young squirrels had met before appearing down in the gardens of Forest How. From their vantage point, up in the dreys, the squirrels would have been able to watch the comings and goings at Forest How, and plan their visits accordingly.

With the squirrels just about moulted into their summer coats, identification of certain squirrels was proving something of a problem. A 'mystery' squirrel, which I subsequently identified as Bill, looked almost identical to Celia's Daughter from a distance, both having much blonde in their tails. In fact, side on,

I could only identify Bill by virtue of some small ticks around his left eye.

Belinda was the easy one to identify. Some black having appeared in her tail in May which, by June, had turned into a black band near the tip. With the passage of time, would more bands appear? Squirrels moult their head and body fur twice per year, but tail and ear-tufts only once. She had learned a new trick; unable to carry two hazelnuts in her mouth, she had realised that if she opened one, loaded the kernel into her mouth, and used a second nut as a 'stopper', this worked fine and reduced the number of trips which she had to make.

Belinda was seen up in the large beech tree, one day, checking on the prospective autumn crop. In some respects, September might be viewed as the start of the squirrel year.

The woods and fellside rang with the sounds of squirrel calls, and teeth chattering, on a daily basis. In fact I probably heard more squirrel communication, in a few short days, than in all of my previous visits combined. What it all meant, I could only guess; maybe juvenile squirrels and parents keeping in touch from their respective locations. On one occasion, Belinda was happily munching her way through pieces of hazelnut, on the popular feeding log with tail flopped characteristically over her back, and completely ignored the calls.

My short June visit was very tiring. I was up each day by 04:45

(and still missed some early action), with squirrel sightings as late as 21:20 on one day. It did, however, have its rewards. Belinda was not seen until about 19:40 on the first evening, when she arrived at one of the feeding positions close to the bridleway. She decided to eat a few nuts, whilst John and I watched, then suddenly charged off down the bridleway. "Heading for the wood," I said, as I chased off via the shortest route.

I ran across the terrace, the lawn, and through the small orchard, before dropping to a walk on the sleeper boardwalk into Foresthow Wood. There were no sightings as I went. However; when I reached the feeding position, the living tree blown down by a winter gale, there was Belinda standing over the two hazelnuts which I had left. It was almost as if she had her 'arms' crossed, with a "What kept you?" expression on her face. She waited until I had settled, before running off with the first nut; returning with a very muddy nose.

Belle's son, suffering from squirrelpox; 13th June 2015.

Belinda's bold son, 12th June 2015.

Belinda's cute daughter, 15th June 2015.

Belinda's daughter, 15th June 2015. Celia's Grandson charging in.

Belinda, 13th June 2015. Black band now formed.

Chapter 15 – Highs and Lows of Summer

When I commenced writing this book, based mainly on my own observations, I knew, in broad terms when it would end, but not how. I view autumn as the start of the squirrel year, and the book has covered a three year period from the autumn of 2012 to the summer of 2015. I had discussed the idea of a book with John Harris on several occasions, but did not want to produce just a book of 'squirrel pictures'.

Whilst I have concentrated mainly on the highs and lows of the Forest How Red Squirrels colony, John and Deb are closely linked to the fortunes of the squirrels, by virtue of the fact that the squirrels live in locations surrounding the guest house. John has worked tirelessly to give the red squirrels the best possible chance of survival and success with the daily provision of supplementary food. Also, and reluctantly on his part, he has carried out grey squirrel control.

The spring of 2015 saw John diagnosed with a serious illness and, faced with the possibility of several months of reduced activity, set to work producing more squirrel nest boxes, and finally getting around to those 'must do' jobs at the guest house.

The focus of the book then became clear to me; an overview of the squirrel colony during the first two years of my involvement, followed by a third year concentrating mainly on Belinda. This fairly accurately reflected the photographic bias over the three year period.

My July visit was preceded by a few days spent near Keswick. When Deb picked me up from Cockermouth, she mentioned that there had been sightings of a poorly squirrel, dark in colour. I was immediately concerned that this would be another case of squirrelpox, and could work out two possible squirrels. When I arrived at Forest How, late in the afternoon, I was soon greeted by four squirrels. I was a little puzzled not to see Belinda.

Up early, the next morning, I was soon seeing the squirrels arriving for their breakfast. Belinda appeared from the fellside, but not with her usual dynamic approach. She reached the feeding stump, and was immediately chased away by Bill. Going only as far as the largest pine tree, she then returned to the stump. As she arrived at the stump, her left side was on view, but when she turned, my heart sank. Her right eye and right front leg showed what appeared to be signs of advanced squirrelpox.

The life of a red squirrel is not easy. Experts have estimated that 85% fail to see their first birthday. Belinda had achieved that milestone, and successfully bred; producing a son and daughter. The odds on surviving squirrelpox, and other infections which may then be contracted, are very slim.

I had decided that it was high time to name Belinda's offspring. As the squirrels which first appeared in 2014 generally had names beginning with the letter 'B', I had already determined that those appearing in 2015 should have names beginning with 'C'. After some thought, I came up with Charles and Camilla. Already, Charles has been a little star; confident and showing his domination over Celia's Grandson. Whilst Charles lacks Belinda's 'squirrel on a mission' speed and direct movement, he is very agile, and already adept at avoiding Bill in the higher trees. Either Bill or Ben will be his father, but I don't know for certain which.

I am writing this final chapter on a perfect Lakeland summer's day; warm and now sunny, and am sitting in the shade of the garden at Forest How, awaiting the arrival of the squirrels for the 'evening shift'.

Yesterday, I took a good look at Belinda close up, whilst Charles watched on from the large pine tree. Her movement was no worse than on the previous day and, if anything, her eye looked a little better. A while later, she ran across to the small hollow feeding log; hiding inside to avoid Mrs Pheasant, who was also hungry. She then spent much of the day up on the fellside.

Belinda has never ceased to amaze me by the varied locations in which I have found her (or she has found me). This morning, it was in a large oak tree beside the bridleway; south of the guest house. For nearly three years, I have looked at that tree as I walked past, and today was the first time I had seen a squirrel there. I was not overly happy as Belinda climbed through some trees, onto the wall, and down into Foresthow Wood.

It was ages before she appeared in the garden to feed, spending time finding and digging up nuts which she had previously buried. Her eye and leg looked no worse, and she made her way to the feeding stump where John and I watched her take and eat a peanut. Then she was off up the fellside, *her* fellside, bouncing off the trees as she went, in her usual fashion, and with the blonde tip of her tail visible between the clumps of bracken.

Later in the day, Celia's Grandson was being aggressively chased by another squirrel; around a pine tree, then down onto the fellside grass. Round in circles he went, unable to outrun the other squirrel, and finally shot up into a tree, with the chasing squirrel in close pursuit, seeking safety high in the tree. I didn't think that my eyes were deceiving me and, as I drew close to the tree, could see that the other squirrel was Belinda. That squirrel has spirit.

On every occasion when leaving Forest How, I have wondered whether I had seen individual squirrels for the last time. In nature, as in life generally, you can never be certain what tomorrow will bring.

If today is to be the last time I see Belinda, I will have many precious memories of times spent with a wild animal, which put her trust in humans, and in return gave a glimpse of the life of a red squirrel. To have known Belinda has been a real privilege.

As to the future, I hope that the remaining Forest How Red Squirrels remain healthy and, just maybe, I will have the opportunity to study Charles, who, one day, may become the dominant male squirrel.

Belinda, 10th July, looking poorly.

The fellside hollow log, popular with the squirrels.

Belinda flying the flag, 29th November 2014.
Happy to try out a new squirrel prop.

Belinda, posing in the garden, 16th March 2015.

Belinda on the terrace, 27th April 2015.

Belinda's son, Charles; 8th July 2015.

Postscript

Sadly, John Harris died in August 2015. My subsequent visit was extended to include his funeral.

Whilst we don't know what the future holds, Belinda had survived her illness, and appeared to have almost completely recovered. She was bossing her territory and, one morning, took several hazelnuts from my hand.

Belinda looking better, 31st August 2015.

About the author

The seeds were sown, for my interest in red squirrels, back in the summer of 1965. A family get-together was arranged at RHS Wisley. As we greeted each other, in the car park, my father suddenly pointed, and said "Look, a red squirrel!" I can't say that I saw the squirrel, but I certainly saw movement in the branches. At the time, I did not know why my father was so excited; however, more recently, I came to understand that the red squirrel would have been almost extinct, in this part of England, by this date.

Photography has accompanied many of my interests, over the years, documenting moments in time. 2010 saw me in Poole, where I realised that it was possible to visit Brownsea Island on a day trip from home. My first visit saw me watching two red squirrels for about forty minutes, high up in pine trees, engaged in a chase. Whilst my photographs were nothing to get excited about, unnoticed, I managed to creep close to the action. Too close, in fact, since one squirrel used a dead branch as a springboard, only for it to break and fall almost at my feet. Needless to say, I was hooked by these enchanting animals.

I had read that the British Wildlife Centre, in Surrey, had recently opened a walk-through red squirrel enclosure, which might enable me to see and photograph the squirrels close up. I didn't realise how close! The squirrels had become used to visitors, and one was known to use them as trees. One little squirrel, named Cyril, had noted this activity, and I could see that he wanted to jump on me from the boardwalk handrail. I crouched down to his level. Cyril looked to my right shoulder, left shoulder, right shoulder and back. Finally, having decided, he jumped; landing on my head!

Having studied squirrel behaviour at the BWC for more than a year, I turned my attention once again to Brownsea Island, and the Isle of Wight. In 2012, my Forest How study, in Cumbria, commenced.

Technical Data

All squirrel photographs were taken using Sony cameras, with 50mm, 135mm and 300mm lenses. The photographs were taken with manual focus, and mostly hand-held; using a wide aperture, giving a shallow depth of field.